BBC Gardeners' World

POCKET PLANTS

WATER GARDEN PLANTS

Andi Clevely

D0278202

BBC Books

Author Biography
Andi Clevely has been a working gardener for nearly thirty years. He began his career in Leeds City Council central nurseries and since then has worked in many gardens around the country, including Windsor Great Park. He is now responsible for a country estate and large garden in Stratford-on-Avon where he lives with his family. Andi has written a number of gardening books and presents a weekly gardening programme.

Acknowledgements

The publishers would like to thank Barnsdale Gardens, Rutland; Honeysome Aquatic Nursery, near Ely, Cambridgeshire, and Stapeley Water Gardens Ltd, Stapeley, Nantwich, Cheshire, for their assistance with the photography. Photographs by Stephen Hamilton © BBC except the following pages: A–Z Botanical Collection 14 (Adrian Thomas), 41 (Peter Etchells), 63 (J. Malcolm Smith), 78 (Geoff Kidd); Eric Crichton 11; Garden Picture Library 9, 48 (Brian Carter), 21 (Didier Willery), 23 (Jerry Pavia), 24, 79 (Geoff Dann), 28 (Sunniva Harte), 29 (Jacqui Hurst), 35 (Howard Rice), 53 (Joan Dear), 66 (Ron Evans); John Glover 39, 49; Andrew Lawson 51; Clive Nichols 7, 16, 44, 76, 80; Oxford Scientific Films 37 (G. H. Thompson); Photos Horticultural 10, 15, 32, 46, 52, 58, 62, 67, 68, 69, 70; Harry Smith Collection 75; Stapeley Water Gardens 60.

Published by BBC Books, an imprint of BBC Worldwide Limited,
Woodlands, 80 Wood Lane, London W12 0TT

First published 1998
© BBC Worldwide Limited 1998
The moral right of the author has been asserted

ISBN 0 563 38418 2

Artwork by Pond and Giles

Set in Futura

Printed and bound in Belgium by Proost NV
Colour separations by Radstock Reproductions Limited, Midsomer Norton, Avon
Cover printed in Belgium by Proost NV

Planning a Water Garden

 Aquatic Plants

Submerged Plants

Waterside Plants

INTRODUCTION

Aquatic and moisture-loving plants are an essential element of water gardening. They help to maintain the natural balance of a pond and attract wildlife. The range of species is enormous and varied and most are easy to grow.

Planning

If a pond is to stay clean and healthy, a balanced collection of plants is vital for shading areas of the surface, oxygenating the water and suppressing algae. As a rough guide, about one-third of the surface should be covered with floating foliage, while a generous number of submerged plants – one for every 0.09 sq.m (1 sq.ft) – helps limit the algal growth that turns pond water green. Between one-third and a half of the perimeter should be planted with marginal and bog garden species.

Most water plants like full sun, although the majority also thrive in light shade, while others tolerate semi- and even full shade. Most also prefer still water. Some plants are better suited to simple formal surroundings, others to more natural ones, and where appropriate this is mentioned in the entries; if possible plant wildlife ponds with useful nectar or shelter plants.

Plant types

Water plants are grouped in categories according to the place they occupy in the pond landscape. Many plants adapt happily to other positions, but the following is a guide to cultural needs.

Aquatic plants: These can be seen on the pond surface. Deep-water aquatics such as water lilies have their roots at the bottom of the pond with their leaves floating or emerging from the surface; they tend to be vigorous, and most ponds can only accommodate 2–3 specimens. Floating plants or 'floaters' drift freely, but a few root temporarily for part of the season; most disappear in the autumn, surviving winter in various dormant states at the bottom of the pond. Both kinds play a major role in shading the pond.

Submerged plants: These, too, are important elements of a balanced plant community because most are oxygenators, supporting the good health of pond flora and fauna, and helping to maintain water clarity. The whole plant generally lives under water, although parts sometimes appear at or above the surface.

Waterside plants: These vary from species which need to be submerged in shallow water, to others that prefer the damp soil of bog gardens. Many are happy in both conditions, and will spread until they reach the limits of their favoured site. A well-made bog garden offers a range of habitats, from very wet to merely moist; wherever a specific position is critical, this is indicated in the text. Most plants have attractive flowers or foliage; many are vigorous and need cutting back if they become invasive.

Planting

Water garden plants are generally undemanding and trouble-free, provided they are given sufficient moisture for their needs. Most plants are introduced in spring or early summer as the water warms up. Floating species are simply launched on the surface, while submerged species are supplied as bundles of cuttings, bound together and weighted with wire or a strip of lead, and are simply tossed into the water. Bottom-rooting aquatics and marginal plants are grown either in special baskets or direct in the soil, while bog garden species are always planted direct.

Planting in baskets: This method has several advantages: the growth of invasive species is restrained, plants can be positioned at different depths by standing baskets on bricks, and removal for general plant care and attention is relatively simple. Special aquatic compost may be used, or fairly heavy garden soil low in fertilizers and organic matter.

- Line the basket with hessian or fine plastic mesh, and for tall species place stones in the bottom to add stability.

- Fill the basket with soil or compost to about 2.5cm (1in) from the rim, water thoroughly and allow to drain.

- Remove the plant from its pot or bag, and then make a hole in the centre of the basket large enough to accommodate the plant roots comfortably.

- Cover the roots with the compost, firm gently and level the surface. Fill the basket to the brim with a layer of 1cm (½in) gravel, and water thoroughly.

- Gently lower the basket into position, using lengths of stout string tied to each side if the water is deep. Make sure it is at the correct depth, measured by the amount of water above the soil surface.

Planting in soil: This is the normal method in bog gardens and also under water where the pond bottom is covered with a layer of soil at least 10–15cm (4–6in) deep. In wildlife and natural ponds, plants can grow as they would in the wild, but growth can be difficult to control, and the water level may have to be lowered at times for maintenance.

- Make sure bog garden soil is free from weeds. Fork over the site thoroughly and add organic material as recommended.

- Dig out a hole, large enough for the roots to fit comfortably and the same depth as the plant grew previously.

- Replace the soil over the roots, firm in the plant, and water well.

- For immersed plants, mix soil or compost with water to a muddy consistency, and mould this into a 15cm (6in) ball around the roots.

- Wrap the ball in a square of hessian, tying the edges round the neck of the plant, and submerge the rootballed plant into place.

Care

Feeding: Most species grow quickly without further assistance, and feeding is only necessary as indicated in the text. Use special slow-release aquatic tablets, pressed into the compost, for basket plants. Avoid overfeeding bog garden plants, because surplus nutrients draining into the pond encourage algae and 'green water'.

Division: Land plants depend on rainfall and often need our intervention to help them grow, whereas water plants tend to be vigorous and have to be restrained from invading each other's territory. They are best controlled by cutting back excessive growth during the season, and by regular division every few years. Always keep the younger outer segments of divided plants for replanting.

Winter care: Mulching with garden compost, leaf mould or straw helps protect bog garden plants in winter, while aquatics are safe if below freezing level. Tender plants must be kept under glass in trays of moist compost, in a cool but frost-free place.

Acorus calamus Sweet Flag

ACORUS CALAMUS 'VARIEGATUS'

The common name of this attractive marsh plant refers to the pleasant citrus or camphor fragrance of its bruised leaves, which were once strewn on floors and are still used to flavour liqueurs. The plants bear tiny flowers clustered on spikes about 10cm (4in) long, but are grown more for their bold foliage.

Flowering time: Early summer (insignificant).

Foliage: Long, flattened; in large clumps.

Height: 60–90cm (2–3ft).

Spread: 75cm (30in).

Positioning: Full sun or light shade; in very wet bog garden soil or immersed to depth of 20cm (8in).

Care: Plant rhizomes in spring, singly or 38–45cm (15–18in) apart in groups, into soil or in baskets. Cut down dead top growth in late autumn (spring in cold areas). Divide every 3–4 years.

Propagation: Divide large plants or cut rhizomes into 10cm (4in) segments in spring.

Recommended: Plain green species and more compact 'Variegatus'.

Useful tip: The variegated form prefers full sun and immersion to only 10cm (4in).

Related plants: *A. gramineus*, fine tufted leaves 30cm (12in) high: best forms 'Variegatus' (white stripes); 'Ogon' (pink and cream stripes); 'Pusillus' (very dwarf).

Ajuga reptans   Bugle, Carpenter's Herb

Flowering time: Late spring to mid-summer.

Foliage: Round and crinkled; dense spreading mats.

Height: 15cm (6in).

Spread: 30cm (12in).

Positioning: Full sun or shade; in moist fertile bog garden soil; as ground cover, pond edging, among rocks.

Care: Plant in autumn or spring, 15cm (6in) apart and mulch with garden compost. Feed in spring with general fertilizer. Trim in autumn if space is limited. Divide every 3–4 years.

Propagation: Divide rosettes in spring.

Recommended: 'Alba' (white flowers); 'Braunherz' (rich purple); 'Atropurpurea' (bronze-purple leaves); 'Variegata' (cream/white edges); 'Burgundy Glow' (pink, purple, cream, green); 'Multicolor' (bronze, red, green).

Useful tip: Dark forms need sunlight; 'Variegata' colours best in shade.

Related plants: *A. pyramidalis*, smaller, especially in 'Metallica Crispa'.

AJUGA REPTANS 'ATROPURPUREA'

This is a neat and undemanding ground-cover plant for almost any site, but is particularly happy in bog gardens, where it may sometimes become rampant. The variegated foliage is colourful at all times, and hugs the contours of rocks and pond banks. In summer the plants erupt with spikes of blue or white flowers.

Alisma plantago-aquatica Water Plantain

ALISMA PLANTAGO-AQUATICA

The lush foliage of this hardy marginal plant is simple and robust, and gives no hint of the dramatic froth of graceful flowers that appear over a long season. These produce prolific quantities of seeds, which will float and germinate around the pond edges if the seedheads are not removed.

Flowering time: Early summer to early autumn.

Foliage: Rich green and spear-shaped; in rosettes. May float when plants are submerged.

Height: 60–90cm (2–3ft).

Spread: 45cm (18in).

Positioning: Full sun or partial shade; in rich muddy bog garden soil (preferably slightly acid) or immersed to depth of 25cm (10in).

Care: Plant in spring or early summer, 30cm (12in) apart in groups, in baskets or into soil enriched with garden compost or leaf mould. Deadhead to prevent lavish self-seeding. Cut down top growth in late autumn.

Propagation: Divide plants in spring or transplant self-set seedlings while small.

Recommended: Basic species and smaller, pink-flowered var. *parviflorum*.

Useful tip: In larger wildlife ponds, leave the seedheads for foraging birds.

Related plants: *A. lanceolatum*, compact with slimmer leaves, is good in small ponds.

Aponogeton distachyos Water Hawthorn

Flowering time: Late spring; autumn.

Foliage: Long, oval, speckled; evergreen in mild gardens.

Height: Foliage 10cm (4in); flowers 90cm (3ft).

Spread: 90cm (3ft).

Positioning: Full sun or semi-shade; immersed to depth of 30–90cm (1–3ft).

Care: Plant tubers or young plants in spring, in baskets spaced 45cm (18in) apart; in large ponds may be planted into soil. Remove dead leaves that surface in autumn. In cold gardens or shallow ponds, overwinter baskets in moist sand under glass and keep dark.

Propagation: Divide clumps in spring.

Recommended: Basic species; 'Grandiflorum' (larger flowered) is sometimes available.

Useful tip: Grow with *Azolla* (Fairy Moss) for dramatic contrast.

Related plants: *A. desertorum*, syn. *A. krausseanus*, is a larger plant with fragrant white or yellow flowers.

APONOGETON DISTACHYOS

The waxy flowers of this South African plant often appear at unpredictable times, even during a mild winter, and have a sweet scent that is powerful and exciting. Plants are hardy in deeper water, and flower freely in shade. They sometimes produce floating seeds, which germinate easily in submerged pots under glass.

Aruncus dioicus Goat's Beard

ARUNCUS DIOICUS

The elegant foliage and regal stature of goat's beards makes them a popular choice for specimen bog garden plants. Their loosely branched plumes of flowers arch gracefully on strong stems that need no support, and in autumn many varieties develop quite startling leaf tints. (syn. *A. sylvester*.)

Flowering time:	Early and mid-summer.
Foliage:	Fresh green serrated leaflets, on long stems.
Height:	Foliage 90cm (3ft); flowers to 1.8m (6ft).
Spread:	90cm (3ft).
Positioning:	Light to medium shade; in rich moist bog garden soil with plenty of humus.
Care:	Plant in autumn or spring, singly or 75cm (30in) apart. Mulch in late autumn with garden compost or leaf mould; feed in spring with general fertilizer. Cut to the ground in late autumn. Divide every 4–5 years.
Propagation:	Divide clumps in spring or autumn or sow seeds in autumn in a cold frame.
Recommended:	Basic species, compact 'Glasnevin', dwarf 'Kneiffii'. A. 'Zweiweltenkind' (bronze leaves, white flowers).
Useful tip:	Group with astilbes and hostas.
Related plants:	A. aesthifolius, low mounds of fine foliage 23cm (9in) high, which turns red in autumn.

Astilbe Astilbe

Flowering time: Mid- to late summer.
Foliage: Daintily cut and decorative; bronze-red tints.
Height: 60cm–1.2m (2–4ft).
Spread: 45–90cm (18in–3ft).
Positioning: Semi-shade; in moist wild or natural bog gardens.
Care: Plant in autumn or spring, singly or 45cm (18in) apart in groups, in moist soil with plenty of humus. Mulch in spring with garden compost. Divide mature clumps every 3–4 years.
Propagation: Divide plants in autumn or spring.
Recommended: A. × arendsii hybrids such as 'Amethyst', 'Cattleya', 'Fanal' and 'Irrlicht'; later-flowering A. chinensis, especially dwarf var. pumila; semi-dwarf A. simplicifolia hybrids.
Useful tip: Avoid vivid colours in wild situations, and group plants naturally with ferns and water irises.
Related plants: Astilboides tabularis, see Rodgersia tabularis.

ASTILBE × ARENDSII 'AMETHYST'

Even if they did not flower, astilbes would be desirable plants as their light, finely cut foliage remains decorative throughout the growing season. Their flowers last for several weeks, and even remain handsome long after fading. Colours vary from soft pastel shades to vivid pink or purple.

AZOLLA FILICULOIDES

This pretty foliage plant is a miniature fern – not a moss as its name suggests – and is graceful and beguiling in appearance, although with a tendency to spread over-enthusiastically: a single plant can become a 1 sq.m (1 sq.yd) patch in just a single season. Leaf fragments and dormant buds survive cold winters at the bottom of the pond.

Flowering time: Non-flowering.

Foliage: Minute, lacy and overlapping; turns rich red in bright sunlight and in cold autumn weather.

Height: 2.5cm (1in).

Spread: Up to 10cm (4in).

Positioning: Surface of still water.

Care: Distribute plants on the pond surface in mid-spring. In nutrient-rich water, plants multiply rapidly and may need thinning with a net in late summer. Overwinter plantlets in a jar of soil and water under glass, or allow them to regenerate naturally.

Propagation: Usually spontaneous. Frond fragments will multiply in water.

Recommended: Basic species only.

Useful tip: Do not introduce into larger inaccessible ponds as plants may become invasive.

Related plants: *A. caroliniana*, sometimes regarded as the same plant, or synonymous with the smaller species *A. mexicana*; leaves remain green and do not overlap.

Butomus umbellatus Flowering Rush

Flowering time: Early to late summer.
Foliage: Rush-like, triangular in section; purplish when young.
Height: 1.2m (4ft).
Spread: 60cm (2ft).
Positioning: Full sun or semi-shade; in muddy bog garden soil or immersed to depth of 15cm (6in).
Care: Plant in spring, into soil or in baskets, 23cm (9in) apart in groups of 5–6 for best effect. Cut down top growth in autumn. Divide plants every 3–4 years otherwise flowering may decline.
Propagation: Divide rhizomes in spring or transplant small bulbs from the sides of mature rhizomes.
Recommended: Basic species; a good white form 'Scheeweissen' is sometimes available.
Useful tip: Combine with reeds, rushes and *Sagittaria* to create a natural waterside community. The flowers dry well and can be used for indoor decoration.
Related plants: None.

BUTOMUS UMBELLATUS

This attractive tall marginal is happiest on the margins of pools and ponds. As its alternative name water gladiolus suggests, it bears distinctive large pink flowers, which are followed by numerous floating seeds that may be sown when ripe. Plants are widely cultivated in Asia for their edible roots.

CALLA PALUSTRIS

This member of the arum family provides perfect ground cover for softening and disguising the bare edges of a pond. Plants eventually form large colonies that look lush and satisfying all season, particularly when they are studded with their 8cm (3in) long white flowers and, later, heads of bright red berries.

Flowering time: Late spring to mid-summer.

Foliage: Thick, glossy and heart-shaped; forms a dense mat. Semi-evergreen in sheltered gardens.

Height: 15–30cm (6–12in).

Spread: 30cm (12in).

Positioning: Full sun or semi-shade; in muddy bog garden soil or immersed to depth of 15cm (6in).

Care: Plant in spring, into the soil of larger ponds or in baskets, singly or 23cm (9in) apart in groups. Cut down dead top growth in late autumn. Divide plants every 4–5 years.

Propagation: Divide rhizomes in spring and replant immediately or, in a cold year, start into growth in trays of mud under glass. Sow seeds in autumn, in situ or in trays of wet compost.

Recommended: Basic species only.

Useful tip: As with all members of the arum family, the berries are poisonous.

Related plants: *Calla aethiopica*, see *Zantedeschia aethiopica*.

Camassia leichtlinii Quamash

Flowering time: Early and mid-summer.

Foliage: Long, strap-like; in neat clumps.

Height: 90cm (3ft).

Spread: 30cm (12in).

Positioning: Full sun or very light shade; in moist but not waterlogged bog garden soil.

Care: Plant bulbs in early or mid-autumn, 10cm (4in) deep and 10–15cm (4–6in) apart in natural patches. Water in dry weather and feed each spring with bonemeal. Allow foliage to die down naturally.

Propagation: Divide clumps in autumn.

Recommended: Basic species, white 'Alba', larger flowered 'Electra', double 'Semiplena' and 'Plena'.

Useful tip: Plants multiply slowly and are best left undisturbed; flowering bulbs can be raised from the plentiful seeds in 3–4 years.

Related plants: *C. cusickii*, early flowering, pale blue; *C. quamash*, syn. *C. esculenta*, blooms open simultaneously.

CAMASSIA LEICHTLINII

Sometimes known as wild hyacinths, Camassias are long-lived bulbs that relish the moist soil of bog gardens. They are best suited to wildlife ponds and natural areas where they can slowly develop into informal drifts. The star-like flowers are blue, white or violet, and open from the bottom of the stout stems.

CARDAMINE PRATENSIS

This charming spring flower of damp meadows and marshes is ideal for planting in a wildlife bog garden. The sprays of dainty blooms look almost white from a distance, although they are a delicate pink with darker veining. Plants may take time to establish, but once happy will spread freely.

Flowering time:	Mid-spring to early summer.
Foliage:	Ferny, pale and delicate; in thick tufts.
Height:	30–45cm (12–18in).
Spread:	30cm (12in).
Positioning:	Light or semi-shade; in damp or marshy bog garden soil, especially among wild flowers and grasses.
Care:	Plant in autumn, 23cm (9in) apart in small groups. Mulch in early spring with garden compost or leaf mould. Allow to die down naturally. Thin vigorous colonies of congested plants.
Propagation:	Divide clumps in late autumn or sow seeds in a cold frame in late summer.
Recommended:	Basic species; also double forms 'Edith', 'Flore Pleno' and 'William'.
Useful tip:	The leaves are an old salad herb, rich in vitamin C; they will root if laid on the surface of moist compost.
Related plants:	*C. raphanifolia*, larger plants and later flowers.

Carex elata 'Aurea' Tufted Sedge

Flowering time: Summer (insignificant).

Foliage: Long, arching; in dense tufts.

Height: 45cm (18in).

Spread: 60cm (24in).

Positioning: Full sun or very light shade; in moist or wet bog garden soil or immersed to depth of 5cm (2in).

Care: Plant in autumn or spring, 30cm (12in) apart in small groups. Feed in spring with bonemeal or general fertilizer. Leave the dry foliage over winter and cut back in early spring. Divide every 5–6 years.

Propagation: Divide clumps in autumn or spring.

Recommended: This is the best form; also variegated 'Knightshayes'.

Useful tip: Use as a pond-edging plant to stabilize soil banks.

Related plants: *C. morrowii* 'Variegata', cream-edged leaves; *C. ornithopoda* 'Variegata', dwarf with white markings; *C. riparia* 'Variegata', green leaves with creamy white stripes.

CAREX ELATA 'AUREA'

This golden form of *Carex elata* is a spectacular alternative to the plain green species, shorter than most other kinds and non-invasive. Although plants are happiest in wet soil or very shallow water, they tolerate temporary droughts, making them the ideal choice for drier bog gardens. (syn. *C. stricta* 'Bowles' Golden'.)

CORNUS ALBA 'SIBIRICA'

An important and vigorous bog garden shrub, this quickly develops into a thicket of coloured stems that provide winter colour and drama, especially where they are reflected in still water. Regular pruning produces maximum bark colour and keeps the naturally large shrubs more compact.

Flowering time:	Early summer.
Foliage:	Green or variegated, on suckering stems; fine autumn tints.
Height:	Up to 2–3m (6½–10ft).
Spread:	Up to 3m (10ft).
Positioning:	Full sun (semi-shade for golden forms); in moist bog garden soil where stems are reflected in water.
Care:	Plant in autumn or spring, singly or 90cm (3ft) apart, in deeply dug soil enriched with garden compost. Cut green-leafed varieties almost to ground level in early spring; prune one-third of variegated shrubs to the ground each year to renew the stems, then feed with general fertilizer.
Propagation:	Take hardwood cuttings in autumn or layer in spring.
Recommended:	Cultivated forms such as 'Aurea', 'Sibirica', 'Spaethii' and 'Westonbirt'.
Useful tip:	Cut out plain green shoots from variegated forms.
Related plants:	*C. stolonifera* 'Flaviramea', greenish-yellow stems.

Cotula coronopifolia
Brass Buttons, Golden Buttons

Flowering time: Early summer to mid-autumn.

Foliage: Fine and aromatic; in spreading clumps.

Height: 15–20cm (6–8in).

Spread: 30cm (12in).

Positioning: Full sun; in very moist bog garden soil, pond-side rockeries or immersed to depth of 10cm (4in).

Care: Sow seeds in mid-spring, under glass in trays of moist compost, and prick out into small pots. Transplant in early summer 15–20cm (6–8in) apart. In very mild gardens, plants may survive the winter and should be divided every 3–4 years.

Propagation: Sow seeds or divide plants in spring.

Recommended: Basic species only; cream-coloured form 'Cream Buttons' occasionally available.

Useful tip: Cuttings taken in autumn will often survive the winter under glass.

Related plants: *C. dioica* and *C. squalida* (both now classed as *Leptinella*) are good ground cover for moist soils.

COTULA CORONOPIFOLIA

This pretty and dependable carpeting plant is a short-lived perennial in very mild gardens, but elsewhere it behaves as a tender annual. Just one sowing is usually sufficient to establish plants because they self-seed freely – though without ever becoming invasive.

Cyperus longus Sweet Galingale

CYPERUS LONGUS

This is a close relative of papyrus and the familiar umbrella plant (commonly grown as a house plant). The hardiest kinds, with their creeping roots, are ideal for planting near pond banks to stabilize the soil. They can become invasive when happy.

Flowering time: Early summer to early autumn.

Foliage: Wide, ribbed, olive green; in whorls on stiff stems.

Height: 90cm (3ft) or more.

Spread: 30–45cm (12–18in).

Positioning: Full sun; in heavy wet bog garden soil or immersed to depth of 15cm (6in).

Care: Plant in autumn or spring, into muddy soil or in baskets. Feed with general fertilizer in spring. Remove any dry stems, and cut down damaged top growth in winter. Divide every 4–5 years.

Propagation: Divide clumps in spring.

Recommended: Basic species only.

Useful tip: Plants also grow from terminal tufts of leaves laid on moist sand or inverted in water.

Related plants: *C. eragrostis* is suitable for bog gardens; grow the barely hardy *C. involucratus* as a house plant or in indoor ponds; dwarf *C. papyrus* 'Nanus', syn. *C. haspan*, for small formal ponds and tubs.

Darmera peltata Umbrella Plant

Flowering time:	Early and mid-spring.
Foliage:	Rounded like upturned parasols; bright copper tints in autumn.
Height:	90cm–1.2m (3–4ft).
Spread:	90cm (3ft).
Positioning:	Full sun or semi-shade; as ground cover in larger moist bog gardens, close to the water's edge.
Care:	Plant in spring, in well-dug soil with plenty of garden compost and a dressing of bonemeal. Feed every spring with general fertilizer and mulch with compost. Deadhead faded blooms and cut down top growth in late autumn. Divide and replant every 4–5 years.
Propagation:	Divide the fleshy roots in spring.
Recommended:	Basic species; also dwarf 'Nana', a perfect miniature only 38cm (15in) high and therefore suitable for small ponds.
Useful tip:	Grow with astilbes, ferns and hostas; 'Nana' with small grasses, rushes and sedges.
Related plants:	None.

DARMERA PELTATA

A single specimen of this unusual perennial will cover a large area of ground and provide a long season of interest. The flowers open on strong stems before the appearance of the handsome leaves, which are large, often more than 38cm (15in) across, and arranged in dramatic mounds. (syn. *Peltiphyllum peltatum*.)

21

Eichornia crassipes Water Hyacinth

EICHORNIA CRASSIPES

A beautiful floating plant that is sometimes called water orchid in reference to its large sprays of lavishly marked flowers. In warm climates it spreads rapidly and can become a serious menace, but frost normally controls its growth in temperate gardens. (syn. *Pontederia crassipes*.)

Flowering time: Mid-summer to early autumn.

Foliage: Thick and succulent, with buoyant inflated stems.

Height: 20–30cm (8–12in).

Spread: Up to 90cm (3ft).

Positioning: Full sun; on pond surface.

Care: Plant in late spring or early summer by dropping individual plants into the water. In a hot season plants may need thinning out to control their spread. In autumn transfer a few young plants to an indoor aquarium or keep in trays of wet soil in a greenhouse.

Propagation: Separate young plants from their runners in spring, or in autumn if plants are housed in a heated aquarium or greenhouse, minimum 14°C (57°F), with supplementary lighting in mid-winter.

Recommended: Basic species only.

Useful tip: Cool dull summers and heavy shade can suppress flowering.

Related plants: *E. azurea* and *E. paniculata*, tender plants for indoor ponds only.

Equisetum hyemale Scouring Rush

Flowering time: Early summer (insignificant).

Foliage: Stiff stems with swollen joints; no obvious leaves.

Height: 60cm–1.2m (2–4ft).

Spread: 30cm (12in).

Positioning: Full sun or light shade; in moist or wet bog garden soil or immersed to depth of 15cm (6in).

Care: Plant in autumn or spring, in baskets under water or in large pots buried in the soil. No further attention is needed, except to cut off dead stems. Divide every 4–5 years.

Propagation: Divide creeping roots in summer.

Recommended: Basic species; also var. robustum, syn. E. robustum, taller, semi-evergreen.

Useful tip: Always confine plants: unrestricted roots can spread 5m (15ft) or more.

Related plants: Many other species are suitable, including E. variegatum with black, green and orange tips, semi-dwarf E. arvense and very dwarf E. scirpoides.

EQUISETUM HYEMALE

All the horsetails are ancient plants whose decomposition produced coal. This species is one of the most attractive for garden ponds, provided its creeping rhizomes can be prevented from spreading extensively. The stems contain silica and were once used to polish metal, hence the common name.

23

Eriophorum angustifolium Cotton Grass

ERIOPHORUM ANGUSTIFOLIUM

Acid peatbogs and moorland marshes are the natural habitats of this outstanding sedge. Modest and elegant for much of the year, it is a highlight in summer when the long silky fibres of its nodding seedheads are a memorable sight. It needs an acid environment, so check the acidity of your soil and water before choosing plants.

Flowering time: Mid-spring to early summer.

Foliage: Slim, drooping; in neat clumps.

Height: 45–75cm (18–30in).

Spread: 30cm (12in).

Positioning: Full sun or semi-shade; in wet acid bog garden soil or immersed to depth of 10cm (4in).

Care: Plant in spring, 23cm (9in) apart in small groups, into the soil or in baskets of lime-free compost. Feed with an ericaceous (lime-free) fertilizer in spring and mulch plants on land with garden compost. Allow flower stems to die down naturally and leave established plants undisturbed.

Propagation: Divide plants in spring.

Recommended: Basic species; 'Heidelicht' is sometimes offered.

Useful tip: Grow in bold drifts at the edge of a wildlife pond to create a natural effect.

Related plants: *E. latifolium* (Broad-leafed Cotton Grass) is very similar, but tolerates lime in soil or water.

Eupatorium cannabinum Hemp Agrimony

Flowering time: Late summer to mid-autumn.

Foliage: Serrated and spear-shaped, on red stems.

Height: Up to 1.5m (5ft).

Spread: 60–75cm (24–30in).

Positioning: Full sun or light shade; in a moist bog garden or immersed to depth of 10cm (4in).

Care: Plant in spring, singly or 45cm (18in) apart in groups of 2–3, into the soil or in a large basket. Feed in spring with general fertilizer. Deadhead to prevent excessive seeding. Cut down top growth in late autumn.

Propagation: Divide plants in spring or transplant self-set seedlings.

Recommended: Basic species, double 'Flore Pleno' and white-flowered 'Album'.

Useful tip: Plants are a good source of nectar for grazing butterflies.

Related plants: *E. purpureum* (Joe Pye Weed), especially dark-leafed 'Atropurpureum' and ssp. *maculatum* with deep purple flowers.

EUPATORIUM CANNABINUM

The impressive stature of this robust plant makes it an ideal choice for growing beside larger wildlife ponds, where it can cast stunning reflections in the water. The downy flowers will attract bees and other foraging insects. Plants self-seed freely unless spent flowers are removed.

FILIPENDULA KAMTSCHATICA ROSEA

The foliage alone would justify including this hardy meadow plant in a bog garden, where the constantly moist conditions encourage lush leafy bushes that are quite wind-resistant. The dense froth of blossom is the plant's real glory, however, with a sweet perfume that lingers in the summer sunshine.

Flowering time: Early summer to early autumn.

Foliage: Deeply cut, rich green or gold; on branching bushes.

Height: Up to 1.5m (5ft).

Spread: 90cm–1.2m (3–4ft).

Positioning: Full sun or semi-shade; in moist rich bog garden soil.

Care: Plant in autumn or spring, singly or 60cm (2ft) apart in groups, in deeply dug ground enriched with garden compost. In spring feed with general fertilizer and mulch with compost. Cut down dead top growth in late autumn.

Propagation: Divide creeping roots in winter or early spring.

Recommended: *F.ulmaria*, golden 'Aurea' (in shade only) and double 'Flore Pleno'.

Useful tip: Position plants to stand out against the water and blue skies.

Related plants: *F. palmata*, *F. rubra*, *F. kamtschatica rosea* and their various cultivated forms are similar, with pink or red flowers.

Fritillaria meleagris Snakeshead Fritillary

Flowering time: Mid- to late spring.

Foliage: Slender and arching; in thin tufts.

Height: 30–38cm (12–15in).

Spread: 10–15cm (4–6in).

Positioning: Full sun or semi-shade; in a moist but not waterlogged bog garden or pond-side rockery.

Care: Plant in autumn, 5–8cm (2–3in) deep and 15cm (6in) apart in groups and drifts. Feed with general fertilizer in spring. Allow foliage to die down naturally. Clumps develop slowly and need division only after many years.

Propagation: Divide mature clumps in late summer, or grow on small offsets from main bulbs in pots of moist compost.

Recommended: Basic species, white forms 'Aphrodite' and *alba*, and 'Artemis', 'Charon', 'Contorta', 'Pomona', 'Saturnus'.

Useful tip: Handle the fragile bulbs carefully; do not allow them to dry out.

Related plants: *F. pallidiflora*, light yellow, for moist soils; prefers semi-shaded positions.

FRITILLARIA MELEAGRIS

Most fritillaries thrive in hot dry positions, in full sun, but a few species are found naturally in moist meadows and are therefore ideal for planting in a bog garden where other bulbs would decline. Grow fritillaries in bold masses – their chequered nodding heads are unique and always eye-catching.

GENTIANA PNEUMONANTHE

This gentian is an essential bog garden plant, for no other species contributes such an intense shade of blue to colour compositions. It is a wild plant from acid marshes, and needs similarly moist lime-free conditions. Grow with sedges and ferns for maximum impact.

Flowering time: Late summer.

Foliage: Lush and shiny, on short slender stems.

Height: 30cm (12in).

Spread: 25–30cm (10–12in).

Positioning: Full sun or light shade; in rich moist bog garden soil that is completely lime-free.

Care: Plant in spring, 15–20cm (6–8in) apart in small groups, in soil enriched with garden compost. Mulch in spring with compost or leaf mould. If leaves turn yellow, water plants every year with sequestered iron to restore their acidity levels.

Propagation: Take cuttings in summer and root in heat or sow seeds in spring under glass.

Recommended: Basic species only.

Useful tip: Plants resent disturbance, so do not move them once established.

Related plants: Taller *G. asclepiadea* (Willow Gentian) tolerates some lime in the soil; blue, white and pink forms are available.

Geum rivale Water Avens

Flowering time: Late spring to mid-summer.

Foliage: Rich green, lush and irregularly toothed.

Height: 30–45cm (12–18in).

Spread: 45cm (18in).

Positioning: Dappled sunlight or light shade; in a cool place in rich moist bog garden soil.

Care: Plant in autumn or spring, singly or 30cm (12in) apart in small groups, in well-dug and manured soil. Mulch in autumn with garden compost or well-rotted manure; feed in spring with general fertilizer. Cut down top growth in autumn. Divide every 3–4 years.

Propagation: Divide clumps in autumn or spring.

Recommended: Basic species; also many garden forms such as 'Album', 'Dingle Apricot', 'Lionel Cox' and 'Variegatum'.

Useful tip: Combines well with Candelabra primulas.

Related plants: Garden forms such as G. 'Borisii' and G. 'Coppertone' enjoy moist soil and full sun.

GEUM RIVALE

This is a close relative of the more familiar border geums and is a wild flower of damp woods and shady streamsides, although in cultivation it will accept most positions, even full sun. The blooms hang like bells, and their rich colour stands out effectively in the evening light.

Glyceria maxima (Reed) Sweet Grass, Water Grass

GLYCERIA MAXIMA VAR. VARIEGATA

This grass is ideal for bog gardens and pond edges and soon colonizes huge areas of waterside if allowed its freedom. The plain green species is also used for fodder and as a thatching grass; a single plant of the prettily variegated form makes a fine highlight for smaller ponds.

Flowering time:	Mid-summer (insignificant).
Foliage:	Luminous, arching and flexible.
Height:	Up to 1.5m (5ft); flower stems to 2.4m (8ft).
Spread:	60–90cm (2–3ft).
Positioning:	Full sun or light shade; in wet bog garden soil or immersed to depth of 15cm (6in).
Care:	Plant in spring, direct into the soil or in baskets to restrain spread. Feed in spring with half-strength general fertilizer. Cut down fading top growth in late autumn. Divide every 4–5 years.
Propagation:	Divide mature clumps in early spring.
Recommended:	Basic species for wildlife ponds; G. m. var. variegata is smaller and more ornamental.
Useful tip:	Both green and variegated kinds are ideal for stabilizing the banks of running watercourses and larger ponds.
Related plants:	None of garden value.

Gunnera manicata (Giant) Prickly Rhubarb

Flowering time: Late summer.

Foliage: Rich green, up to 3m (10ft) across, on prickly stalks.

Height: 2–3m (6½–10ft).

Spread: 5m (16ft).

Positioning: Full sun or semi-shade with shelter from cold winds; in rich moist bog garden soil.

Care: Plant in late spring, in well-dug soil enriched with garden compost. In spring feed with general fertilizer and mulch the young growth lavishly with compost. Cut down exhausted flower stalks; in autumn cut fading leaves and use them to protect the roots from frost.

Propagation: Divide plants in spring.

Recommended: Basic species; also the slightly smaller *G. tinctoria* (Giant Chilean Rhubarb).

Useful tip: Plants can tolerate light frost and in mild sheltered gardens will remain evergreen.

Related plants: Miniature *G. magellanica*, 10–15cm (4–6in) high and 60–90cm (2–3ft) wide, is ideal for small ponds.

GUNNERA MANICATA

A vigorous and magnificent waterside plant that can add an exotic flourish to a large bog garden. The huge leaves are spectacular, large enough to shelter beneath, and the 1.8m (6ft) greenish-red flower spikes are equally impressive. Grow with other foliage plants beside large areas of still water.

Helionopsis orientalis Helionopsis

HELIONOPSIS ORIENTALIS VAR. BREVISCARPIA

This attractive Japanese perennial is a relative newcomer to western bog gardens. The nodding dainty flowers are borne in groups on strong stalks and are like those of some woodland bulb, but the plants are actually evergreen perennials. Their roots resent disturbance.

Flowering time: Mid- to late spring.

Foliage: Spear-shaped; in ground-hugging rosettes.

Height: 23–30cm (9–12in).

Spread: 15cm (6in).

Positioning: Semi-shade or dappled sunlight; in moist rich bog garden soil.

Care: Plant in spring, 10–15cm (4–6in) apart in small groups, in ground enriched with garden compost or leaf mould. Feed in spring with general fertilizer and mulch. In very cold gardens, protect plants in autumn with a layer of leaves or bracken.

Propagation: Divide plants in spring and grow on in pots until rooted; sow seeds in late summer in a cold frame.

Recommended: Basic species; also var. *breviscarpa* (white flowers and plantlets at leaf ends).

Useful tip: Plants need a season or two to establish and should not be disturbed. Grow near the water, at the base of taller perennials and shrubs.

Related plants: None.

Flowering time: Early to late summer.
Foliage: Narrow and arching; in sturdy clumps.
Height: 45cm–1.2m (18in–4ft).
Spread: 45–60cm (18–24in).
Positioning: Full sun; in moist rich bog garden soil.
Care: Plant in autumn or spring, 45–60cm (18–24in) apart in groups of 3 or more, in soil enriched with garden compost or well-rotted manure. Mulch with compost in autumn; feed each spring with general fertilizer. Cut down top growth in late winter. Divide every 3–5 years.
Propagation: Divide plants in autumn or spring.
Recommended: Many good cultivars including 'Anzac', 'Black Prince', 'Franz Hals', 'Golden Chimes', 'Sammy Russell'.
Useful tip: New plants need 2–3 seasons to produce their best display.
Related plants: *H. citrina* and *H. lilioasphodelus*, elegant yellow species, both fragrant.

HEMEROCALLIS 'FRANZ HALS'

Each day-lily stem carries up to 40 buds that open in succession so, although the beautiful blooms last for only a day, the plants give a prolonged and stunning display. They adapt to many garden sites, but are happiest in a bog garden, where their prolific foliage looks fresh and decorative all season.

HOSTA FORTUNEI 'FRANCEE'

Hostas are the ultimate foliage plants for bog gardens, revelling in the damp conditions and even tolerating full sun if the soil is very moist. Leaf colours range from blue-green to gold, often with white or cream markings, and the white or mauve flowers are subtly perfumed.

Flowering time: Early summer to early autumn.

Foliage: Large, oval and pointed; in a wide range of colours.

Height: 30–60cm (1–2ft).

Spread: 45cm (18in) or more.

Positioning: Full or semi-shade; in rich moist bog garden soil.

Care: Plant in spring, singly or 38cm (15in) apart in small groups, in deeply dug and well-manured or composted ground. Feed in spring with general fertilizer and mulch with compost. Remove faded flowers and leaves. Slug and snail control is important at all times.

Propagation: Divide plants in spring.

Recommended: H. decorata, H. fortunei, especially 'Francee', H. undulata, H. lancifolia, H. sieboldiana, H. ventricosa and their varieties.

Useful tip: Plants need 2–3 seasons to become established. Grow with Candelabra primulas and astilbes.

Related plants: None.

Hottonia palustris Water Violet

Flowering time: Early to mid-summer.

Foliage: Ferny; in dense submerged mats.

Height: Flowers 23–38cm (9–15in).

Spread: 75cm (30in).

Positioning: Full sun or light shade; in still, slightly acid water 10–60cm (4–24in) deep.

Care: Plant in spring by dropping individual plants into the water, 5–6 specimens for each square metre to be covered. Thin plants during summer if growth is excessive. Allow plants to die back in autumn: dormant buds and ripe seeds survive the winter on bottom of the pond.

Propagation: Divide plants or take stem cuttings in summer; gather submerged seeds and grow in trays of mud, or transplant seedlings.

Recommended: Basic species only.

Useful tip: Plants do not like agitated water: keep away from fountains and waterfalls.

Related plants: *H. inflata* (Featherfoil) is smaller, with white flowers.

HOTTONIA PALUSTRIS

The main mass of the water violet's oxygenating foliage floats just below the surface, sometimes rooting into mud on the bottom of the pond and then freeing itself at flowering time. The airy spikes of attractive flowers set seeds that continue to ripen all winter under water.

Houttuynia cordata Houttuynia

HOUTTUYNIA CORDATA 'CHAMELEON'

The basic species of this vigorous ground-cover perennial has lush green red-stemmed leaves that provide the perfect foil for its clear white flowers, and is just as attractive as its better-known green, yellow and red variegated form. Growth may be rampant in wet soil, but is easily controlled.

Flowering time: Early and mid-summer.

Foliage: Bold, green or variegated, with a strong peppery aroma when handled; evergreen in mild gardens.

Height: 30–38cm (12–15in).

Spread: 30–45cm (12–18in).

Positioning: Full sun or semi-shade; in moist bog gardens or immersed to depth of 10cm (4in).

Care: Plant in spring, singly or 30cm (12in) apart in groups, into moist soil enriched with garden compost, or in baskets to limit spread. Remove faded leaves in autumn.

Propagation: Divide creeping roots in spring.

Recommended: Basic species and coloured forms 'Chameleon' and *variegata*.

Useful tip: In very cold gardens, overwinter young portions of plants in pots under glass or mulch plants thickly with leaves or bracken.

Related plants: 'Flore Pleno', an attractive flowering form with double blooms like those of a water lily.

Hydrocharis morsus-ranae Frogbit

Flowering time: Early to late summer.

Foliage: Bronze-green kidney-shaped pads float in rosettes.

Height: Flower stems 5–8cm (2–3in).

Spread: 60cm (24in) or more.

Positioning: Preferably sun but plants tolerate shade; on the surface of still water up to 30cm (12in) deep.

Care: Plant in mid-spring: drop plantlets on the pond surface. Growth can be rapid and colonies may need thinning with a net during summer. Plants disappear in winter and survive as dormant buds on the bottom of the pond.

Propagation: Separate plantlets from runners at any time during the year.

Recommended: Basic species only.

Useful tip: In very cold gardens, overwinter a few plantlets under glass in jars of soil and water as an insurance against loss.

Related plants: *Limnobium spongia*, syn. *H. spongia* (American Frogbit), is very similar.

HYDROCHARIS MORSUS-RANAE

A complex botanical name for a charmingly simple floating plant that resembles a miniature water lily. Growth can be invasive in ideal conditions, but the surface coverage can easily be controlled by thinning, even in small ponds. Swollen terminal buds form on stems in autumn and hibernate on the bottom of the pond.

Flowering time: Mid-summer; sometimes again in early autumn.

Foliage: Long, narrow, smooth; sheathed at base.

Height: Up to 60cm (2ft).

Spread: 20–25cm (8–10in).

Positioning: Full sun or very light shade; in marginal mud or immersed to depth of 10cm (4in). Dislikes lime.

Care: Plant in spring or immediately after flowering, 30cm (12in) apart, into the soil or in baskets. Deadhead flower spikes; remove faded leaves in autumn. Divide every 4–5 years.

Propagation: Divide clumps into young root segments after flowering.

Recommended: Basic species and many varieties such as 'Alba', 'Midnight', 'Variegata', 'Cherry Garden'.

Useful tip: Set rhizomes at or just below the soil surface.

Related plants: I. ensata, syn. I. kaempferi (Japanese Flag), I. pseudacorus (Yellow Flag) and I. versicolor (American Blue Flag) are alternative water irises.

IRIS LAEVIGATA 'CHERRY GARDEN'

Irises vary in their needs and the lovely violet-blue Japanese water iris is typical of those that prefer to have their thick rhizomes bathed in water. It has been crossed with *I. ensata* to produce many richly coloured hybrids such as 'Cherry Garden'. All these need acid soil; in alkaline conditions choose *I. pseudacorus* or *I. versicolor*.

Iris sibirica Siberian Iris

Flowering time: Late spring and early summer.

Foliage: Very narrow and upright; in strong tufts.

Height: 75–90cm (30–36in).

Spread: 30cm (12in).

Positioning: Full sun or very light shade; in rich moist bog garden soil.

Care: Plant in early summer, singly or 23cm (9in) apart in groups, no more than 5cm (2in) deep in well-dug soil with plenty of garden compost. Mulch or feed with general fertilizer after flowering each year. Deadhead; clear damaged or faded leaves. Divide every 5–6 years.

Propagation: Divide plants into young segments after flowering.

Recommended: Basic species; also hybrids such as 'Purple Cloak', 'Southcombe White', 'Sparkling Rosé'.

Useful tip: Plants take 1–2 seasons to settle in.

Related plants: *I. orientalis*, syn. *I. ochroleuca*, *I. chrysographes* and *I. innominata* are good bog plants.

IRIS SIBIRICA

These elegant irises are streamside plants and deserve a place beside any garden pond, whether small or large, formal or wildlife. Unlike some other species they tolerate most types of soil, provided it is fairly damp, and come in a range of gorgeous colours and markings.

Juncus effusus Soft Rush

JUNCUS EFFUSUS 'SPIRALIS'

This evergreen rush has brown fruits that are decorative all year round and is usually seen in its bizarre form 'Spiralis', one of the few corkscrew grasses that are available for water gardens. All forms are attractive, however, and their gently rooting growth is ideal for securing the edges of ponds.

Flowering time: Summer.

Foliage: Smooth, cylindrical; in dense tufts.

Height: Up to 60cm (2ft).

Spread: 45cm (18in).

Positioning: Full sun or light shade; in wet bog garden soil or immersed to depth of 10cm (4in).

Care: Plant in spring, 15–20cm (6–8in) apart in groups, into the soil or in baskets. Immersed plants need little care; in spring feed bog garden plants with general fertilizer or mulch with garden compost. Divide every 4–5 years.

Propagation: Divide clumps in late spring or sow seeds in wet compost under glass in late summer.

Recommended: Basic species; also 'Spiralis' (Corkscrew Rush) and variegated 'Cuckoo', 'Vittatus', 'Zebrinus'.

Useful tip: Plant at pond margins to stabilize banks and camouflage edges.

Related plants: *J. conglomeratus*, large seedheads; *J. ensifolius*, flattened leaves, dark brown decorative flowers.

Lagarosiphon major Curly Water Thyme

Flowering time: Summer (minute and insignificant).
Foliage: Curled; closely set in whorls on thin stems.
Height: Submerged only.
Spread: Up to 2.4m (8ft).
Positioning: Full sun or light shade; in water 15–60cm (6–24in) deep.
Care: Plant in spring or summer by tossing small weighted bundles of cuttings into the water. Remove straggly stems after winter.
Propagation: Tie stem cuttings, 10cm (4in) long, in weighted bundles and drop them in the pond in spring and summer.
Recommended: Basic species; also smaller *L. muscoides*, syn. *L. schweinfurtii*, *L. dregeana*, slightly tender with transparent leaves.
Useful tip: Each bundle of stem cuttings can cover a square metre within a year, and may need to be thinned with a fork or rake.
Related plants: *Egeria densa*, syn. *Elodea densa*, very similar; *Elodea canadensis*, popular but invasive and less decorative.

LAGAROSIPHON MAJOR

This is a valuable submerged oxygenator and is also useful for sheltering wildlife, filtering lime from hard water and maintaining a healthy pond. As its alternative name, water weed, suggests, caution is advisable before introducing it in small ponds. (syn. *Elodea crispa*.)

Ligularia dentata Ligularia

LIGULARIA DENTATA 'DESDEMONA'

This bog garden aristocrat forms stately clumps of handsome foliage, enhanced by red or purple tints in some forms. In summer its tall strong stems are crowned by large magnificent flowers in various shades of yellow. Plants enjoy lavish conditions, so feed them well and keep them very moist at all times.

Flowering time: Mid-summer to mid-autumn.

Foliage: Large, rounded or heart-shaped; in spreading clumps.

Height: 90cm–1.5m (3–5ft).

Spread: 90cm (3ft).

Positioning: Dappled sun or light shade, with shelter from strong winds; in rich moist or wet bog garden soil.

Care: Plant in autumn or spring, singly or 75cm (30in) apart, in deeply dug, manured soil. Mulch in autumn with garden compost or well-rotted manure; feed in spring with general fertilizer. Cut back stems after flowering. Divide every 3–4 years.

Propagation: Divide clumps in spring.

Recommended: Basic species and 'Desdemona', 'Othello'.

Useful tip: Grouped plants are effective weed-suppressants.

Related plants: *L. japonica*, bright, star-shaped blooms; *L. przewalskii*, lemon yellow, black stems; *L. veitchiana*, purple leaves in autumn.

Lobelia cardinalis Cardinal Flower

Flowering time: Mid-summer to early autumn.

Foliage: Narrow and shiny, bronze or reddish-green.

Height: 90cm–1.2m (3–4ft).

Spread: 30cm (12in).

Positioning: Full sun or very light shade; in rich wet bog garden soil or immersed to depth of 15cm (6in).

Care: Plant in mid- to late spring, 25cm (10in) apart in specimen groups, into the soil or in baskets. Deadhead flower stems; cut down all growth in autumn. Mulch plants grown on land with compost or straw; move plants in baskets to containers of water under frost-free glass.

Propagation: Divide plants in spring or take cuttings in summer.

Recommended: Basic species; also hybrids such as 'Dark Crusader', 'Queen Victoria', 'Russian Princess'.

Useful tip: Whole stems last well as cut flowers.

Related plants: *L. siphilitica*, hardy and blue-flowered.

LOBELIA CARDINALIS

This gorgeous perennial is safely hardy in mild gardens, but elsewhere it is sensitive to frost and should be mulched or transplanted indoors for the winter. There are several fine varieties, all of which are happiest when dabbling their roots in water.

43

LYSICHITON AMERICANUS

This spectacular plant needs plenty of space, and is ideal planted in larger bog gardens close to the water where its huge leaves and brilliant 20cm (8in) yellow flower spathes may be mirrored. Plants root very deeply and need a soil-based pond if they are grown at its edge.

Flowering time: Early and mid-spring.

Foliage: Enormous, grass green, leathery; smells of cabbage.

Height: 75–90cm (30–36in).

Spread: 60cm (24in).

Positioning: Full sun or light shade; in deep rich wet bog garden soil or immersed to depth of 10cm (4in).

Care: Plant in spring, singly or 75cm (30in) apart in small groups, in deeply dug soil enriched with garden compost or well-rotted manure. Mulch land plants in autumn with compost or leaf mould for protection and feed with general fertilizer in spring. Cut down all growth in autumn.

Propagation: Remove offsets from runners in spring or transplant self-set seedlings at any time.

Recommended: Basic species only.

Useful tip: Do not disturb established plants, as they will need 1–2 seasons to settle down again.

Related plants: *L. camtschatcensis*, smaller species with white flowers.

Lysimachia punctata Garden Loosestrife

Flowering time: Mid-summer to early autumn.

Foliage: Pointed and clear bright green; mellow orange in autumn.

Height: 60–75cm (24–30in).

Spread: 60cm (24in).

Positioning: Full sun or shade; in rich moist or wet, preferably acid, bog garden soil or immersed to depth of 8cm (3in).

Care: Plant in autumn or spring, singly or 30cm (12in) apart in groups, in well-composted soil. Mulch plants grown on land with garden compost or leaf mould in autumn; feed in spring with an ericaceous (lime-free) fertilizer.

Propagation: Divide clumps immediately after flowering.

Recommended: Basic species only.

Useful tip: Plants grow well beneath large shrubs and deciduous trees.

Related plants: *L. ephemerum*, *L. clethroides* and prostrate *L. nemorum* and *L. nummularia* (Creeping Jenny) all enjoy wet conditions.

LYSIMACHIA PUNCTATA

All the Lysimachias enjoy pondside conditions. The popular garden loosestrife is one of the most vigorous, with strong spires of bright golden flowers, and is sometimes rather invasive. It is very tolerant of shade, but does not like highly alkaline soils.

45

Lythrum salicaria Purple Loosestrife

LYTHRUM SALICARIA 'FIRECANDLE'

This is a tall elegant plant, unrelated to other loosestrifes. Its prolific eye-catching flower spikes come in various shades of pink, red or white and are often 90cm (3ft) long. The blooms are long-lasting and an excellent source of nectar for browsing pond insects.

Flowering time: Mid-summer to early autumn.

Foliage: Narrow and pointed, on tall downy stems.

Height: 90cm–1.5m (3–5ft).

Spread: 45–60cm (18–24in).

Positioning: Full sun or very light shade; in rich wet bog garden soil or temporarily immersed to depth of 15cm (6in).

Care: Plant in autumn or spring, 45cm (18in) apart in groups, in well-cultivated soil with plenty of added garden compost. Mulch plants grown on land in autumn; feed each spring with general fertilizer. Cut back all growth in autumn.

Propagation: Divide clumps in autumn or spring or transplant self-set seedlings at any time.

Recommended: Basic species and more compact varieties such as 'Firecandle', 'Robert', 'The Beacon'.

Useful tip: For maximum impact confine groups to a single colour.

Related plants: *L. virgatum*, more slender growth suitable for small ponds.

Mentha aquatica Water Mint

Flowering time: Mid- and late summer.

Foliage: Aromatic, dark green (deep red in full sun).

Height: 60–90cm (2–3ft).

Spread: 75cm (3ft).

Positioning: Full sun or semi-shade; in rich wet bog garden soil or immersed to depth of 15cm (6in).

Care: Plant in spring, singly or 15cm (6in) apart in groups of 3, into the soil of larger bog gardens, or preferably confined in baskets. Cut down top growth in autumn. Divide every 3–4 years and replant in fresh soil.

Propagation: Divide rooted runners in spring.

Recommended: Basic species; also curled *crispa* and dark-leafed 'Rubra'.

Useful tip: Some authorities consider all forms to be the same plant, which varies in appearance with different habitats.

Related plants: *M. pulegium* (Pennyroyal), creeping species for moist bog gardens; *Preslia cervina*, syn. *M. cervina* (Water Spearmint), slightly tender in shallow ponds and cold water.

MENTHA AQUATICA

Like its familiar herb garden relatives, water mint spreads vigorously and is best planted in large containers for effective control. The leaves and shoot tips can be used for flavouring in the usual way, while the fragrant mauve flowers are popular with bees and hover flies.

Menyanthes trifoliata   Bog Bean, Marsh Trefoil

MENYANTHES TRIFOLIATA

This versatile plant is ideal for growing at the water's edge. Its leafy creeping stems soon disguise a pond liner, and are equally content spreading into shallow water to form large floating colonies. From these, the attractively fringed blooms rise gracefully above the pond surface.

Flowering time: Mid-spring to early summer.

Foliage: Neatly divided into 3 smooth oval leaflets.

Height: 23–30cm (9–12in).

Spread: Up to 50–60cm (20–24in).

Positioning: Full sun or very light shade; in waterlogged acid bog garden soil or immersed to depth of 30cm (12in).

Care: Plant in spring, singly or 30cm (12in) apart, into very wet lime-free soil or in baskets of ericaceous (lime-free) compost. Cut back top growth in autumn. Divide every 4–5 years; sooner if vigorous colonies become congested.

Propagation: Divide creeping rhizomes into rooted segments in spring or sow seeds in trays of mud under glass in spring.

Recommended: Basic species only.

Useful tip: Plants are easily restrained in smaller ponds.

Related plants: *Nephrophyllidium crista-galli,* syn. *M. crista-galli* (Deer Cabbage), similar with smaller flowers.

Mimulus ringens Lavender Musk

Flowering time: Early summer to early autumn.

Foliage: Fresh green, slim and elegant, on very upright stems.

Height: 60–90cm (2–3ft).

Spread: 60cm (2ft).

Positioning: Full sun or semi-shade; at the edge of medium-size ponds in water 5–15cm (2–6in) deep.

Care: Plant in spring, 30–45cm (12–18in) apart in small groups, into pond mud or in baskets. Pinch out the growing tips of young plants to encourage bushiness. Cut down top growth in autumn. Divide every 3–4 years.

Propagation: Divide clumps in spring or take cuttings in summer.

Recommended: Basic species only.

Useful tip: Plants self-seed freely, so deadhead them if seedlings are not welcome.

Related plants: *M. luteus* (Water Musk) enjoys similar conditions; *M. lewisii*, *M. cardinalis* and many garden hybrids grown as annuals are suitable for bog gardens.

MIMULUS RINGENS

Lavender musk is a true aquatic, unlike many kinds of Mimulus which are happiest in moist or wet ground, and prefers to grow with its roots submerged in shallow water. Taller than most of its relatives, it makes a large handsome bush that flowers generously, and can seed with abandon.

Molinia caerulea Moor Grass

MOLINIA CAERULEA 'VARIEGATA'

This hardy perennial grass is decorative all year round and also tough enough to withstand drought, a remarkable quality in a water plant. The supple leaves of the plain form look faintly blue from a distance, while variegated kinds are attractive all year round.

Flowering time: Mid-summer to early autumn.

Foliage: Supple and tufted; often variegated or semi-evergreen.

Height: 75cm (30in).

Spread: 50cm (20in).

Positioning: Full sun or very light shade; in moist or wet acid bog garden soil or immersed to depth of 10cm (4in).

Care: Plant in spring, 23–30cm (9–12in) apart in generous drifts, in soil with plenty of garden compost or leaf mould. Mulch land plants in autumn; feed in spring with general fertilizer. Tidy leaves after winter.

Propagation: Divide clumps in spring.

Recommended: Basic species; also subspecies *caerulea* with forms such as 'Moorhexe' (black flowers), 'Variegata' (striped leaves).

Useful tip: Plants can survive drought and total submersion.

Related plants: *Sesleria autumnalis* and *S. heufleriana* both grow well in alkaline soils.

Myrica gale Bog Myrtle, Sweet Gale

Flowering time: Early and mid-spring.
Foliage: Green, tinted red; highly aromatic.
Height: Up to 1.8m (6ft); growth is slow.
Spread: 1.2–1.8m (4–6ft).
Positioning: Light or semi-shade; in moist or wet acid bog garden soil with plenty of humus.
Care: Plant while dormant (late autumn to early spring) in well-dug soil with plenty of garden compost or leaf mould. Mulch in autumn; feed in spring with high-potash fertilizer. Prune lightly to shape after flowering and cut out weak stems at ground level.
Propagation: Take cuttings in summer or sow seeds in ericaceous (lime-free) compost in late summer.
Recommended: Basic species only.
Useful tip: Both the berries and foliage are used for flavouring and medicinal purposes.
Related plants: M. californica (California Wax Myrtle) and M. pensylvanica (Swamp Candleberry) are evergreen or semi-evergreen.

MYRICA GALE

This fascinating bog garden shrub has several seasons of interest, starting with the golden catkins that appear on its bare branches in spring. The foliage is irresistibly fragrant, while the tiny yellow-brown berries are dotted with an aromatic resin that is used to make scented candles.

Myriophyllum aquaticum Water Milfoil

MYRIOPHYLLUM AQUATICUM

There are several milfoils, all of which are fine oxygenating plants with attractive ferny leaves; M. aquaticum is the most popular, with very dense foliage that emerges stiffly from the water. It is a tropical species and tends to die back in winter to submerged dormant crowns, which usually revive again in spring.

Flowering time:	Early summer to early autumn.
Foliage:	Finely divided in regularly spaced whorls; forms a deep thick carpet.
Height:	30cm (12in) above water.
Spread:	Up to 1.8m (6ft).
Positioning:	Full sun or light shade; in water 10–60cm (4–24in) deep.
Care:	Plant in late spring or summer by tossing young weighted plants into the water where they are required to grow. Take a few cuttings in late summer and overwinter in wet soil under frost-free glass as an insurance.
Propagation:	Tie 12–15cm (5–6in) cuttings in weighted bundles and drop in the water in spring or summer.
Recommended:	Basic species only.
Useful tip:	Plants may be grown in baskets of wet compost for easy removal under glass in autumn.
Related plants:	M. verticillatum (Whorled Milfoil) and M. spicatum (Spiked Milfoil) are very hardy.

Narthecium ossifragum Bog Asphodel

Flowering time: Mid- and late summer.

Foliage: Narrow and orange-tinted; in flat tufts.

Height: 15–23cm (6–9in).

Spread: 15cm (6in).

Positioning: Full sun; in wet bog garden soil or immersed in water no more than 2.5cm (1in) deep.

Care: Plant in mid-spring, 10cm (4in) apart in generous drifts, in soil with plenty of rotted leaf mould. Plants need little attention until clumps become congested, when they should be divided and replanted in fresh soil.

Propagation: Divide creeping rhizomes in spring or sow seeds in muddy compost in a cold frame in spring.

Recommended: Basic species only.

Useful tip: In cold gardens or where ponds tend to freeze, plant in a bog garden and mulch with leaf mould to ensure that plants survive the winter.

Related plants: N. americanum (Yellow Asphodel) and N. asiaticum, both larger species.

NARTHECIUM OSSIFRAGUM

This plant for the wildlife pond and bog garden is a native of wet heaths and marshes where it grows in large patches and drifts, immersed in very shallow water in summer. Although plants spread steadily, they are sufficiently restrained to grow beside small ponds.

NYMPHAEA 'ATTRACTION'

The ultimate in aquatic plants, these large water lilies only prosper in deep, spacious surroundings. It is easy to be seduced by their outstanding beauty, but assess varieties with care and match their vigour to the size of the pond. Although plants are well out of sight during winter, they are very hardy below ice level.

Flowering time: Late spring to mid-autumn.

Foliage: Rounded or oval, often marbled or variegated; floats at surface level.

Height: More or less at surface level.

Spread: 1.5–2.4m (5–8ft); coverage up to 4.5 sq.m (50 sq.ft).

Positioning: Full sun; in still water at least 45–90cm (1½–3ft) deep.

Care: Plant in late spring or early summer in 20–30cm (8–12in) of bottom mud or in baskets. Lower baskets as leaves grow until full depth is reached (3–4 weeks). Deadhead if possible; remove decaying leaves. Divide every 4–5 years.

Propagation: Divide rhizomes at planting time.

Recommended: 'Attraction' (red), 'Gladstoniana' (white), 'Colonel A J Welch' (yellow), 'Mrs Richmond' (pink) are easy and prolific.

Useful tip: Naturalize lilies in an earth bottom in the deepest ponds to reduce maintenance.

Related plants: None.

Nymphaea   Water Lily (medium)

Flowering time: Late spring to mid-autumn.

Foliage: Rounded or oval, often marbled or variegated; floats at surface level.

Height: More or less at surface level.

Spread: 1.2–1.5m (4–5ft); coverage up to 1.8 sq.m (20 sq.ft).

Positioning: Full sun; in still water 30–60cm (1–2ft) deep.

Care: Plant in late spring or early summer in 20–30cm (8–12in) of bottom mud or baskets. Lower baskets as leaves grow until full depth is reached (3–4 weeks). Deadhead if possible; remove decaying leaves. Divide every 4–5 years.

Propagation: Divide rhizomes at planting time.

Recommended: 'Albatross' (white); 'Atropurpurea' (deep crimson); 'Madame Wilfron Gonnère'.

Useful tip: To plant in deeper ponds with a soil bottom, roll and tie the rhizome in turf and toss into the water.

Related plants: None.

NYMPHAEA 'MADAME WILFRON GONNÈRE'

Moderately large water lily varieties include the ones most commonly seen floating on informal ponds where the plants can spread to their full size. The choice is enormous, with every colour on the palette represented in single, semi-double and double forms.

Nymphaea Water Lily (miniature or dwarf)

NYMPHAEA TETRAGONA (SYN. 'PYGMAEA ALBA')

For miniature ponds and containers such as half-barrels it is best to choose naturally dwarf varieties. These resemble their larger cousins in all but size, and planting them in small baskets limits growth even further in restricted spaces. Winter protection may be necessary because crowns are not covered by a sufficient depth of water.

Flowering time: Late spring to mid-autumn.

Foliage: Rounded or oval, often marbled or variegated; floats on surface.

Height: Surface level.

Spread: 30–60cm (12–24in); coverage up to 0.4 sq.m (4 sq.ft).

Positioning: Full sun; in still water 10–25cm (4–10in) deep.

Care: Plant in late spring or early summer in at least 5cm (2in) of bottom mud or in baskets. Lower baskets to full depth in 2–3 stages. Deadhead; remove fading leaves. Divide every 3–4 years.

Propagation: Divide rhizomes at planting time.

Recommended: 'Aurora' (yellow-orange); 'Helvola' (yellow); 'Paul Hariot' (yellow/red); 'Laydekeri Lilacea' (lilac pink); *N. tetragona*, syn. 'Pygmaea Alba' (white).

Useful tip: Wrap containers in bubble plastic to protect lilies from severe frosts.

Related plants: None.

Flowering time: Late spring to mid-autumn.

Foliage: Rounded or oval, often marbled or variegated; floats on surface.

Height: Surface level.

Spread: Up to 60cm (2ft); coverage up to 1.1 sq.m (12 sq.ft).

Positioning: Full sun; in still water 15–45cm (6–18in) deep.

Care: Plant in late spring or early summer in at least 8cm (3in) of bottom mud or in baskets. Lower baskets to full depth in 2–3 stages. Deadhead; remove fading leaves. Divide every 3–4 years.

Propagation: Divide rhizomes at planting time.

Recommended: 'Caroliniana' (pale pink); 'Ellisiana' (orange); 'Laydekeri Purpurata' (crimson); *N. candida* (white); 'Odorata Sulphurea Grandiflora' (yellow); 'Rose Arey' (pink); 'Sioux' (golden-orange).

Useful tip: These varieties can be grown in tubs and other containers.

Related plants: None.

NYMPHAEA 'SIOUX'

The water lilies listed here include some of the loveliest varieties, with blooms often 15cm (6in) across. Grow them in a small shallow pool – the limited area can be an asset as the water warms quickly, favouring early and prolonged flowering.

ORONTIUM AQUATICUM

Although this distinctive plant will grow as a marginal at the edge of ponds, it is much happier and looks spectacular isolated in deeper water, from which its leaves and bright golden flower spikes erupt dramatically. Quite distinctive, it is worth a prominent position in ponds of every size.

Flowering time: Mid-spring to early summer.

Foliage: Lance-shaped and almost succulent; erect in shallow water, otherwise floating or submerged.

Height: 30–45cm (12–18in).

Spread: 45–60cm (18–24in).

Positioning: Full sun or very light shade; in deep wet soil or immersed to depth of 10–45cm (4–18in).

Care: Plant dormant rhizomes in winter or young plants in spring, into soil at the water's edge or in baskets if immersed. Keep well away from vigorous neighbours which can overwhelm the plants. In autumn mulch plants grown on land with leaf mould and clear dead top growth.

Propagation: Divide plants or take root cuttings in spring.

Recommended: Basic species only.

Useful tip: Plants seldom need division, and should only be disturbed for propagation or if baskets become overgrown.

Related plants: None.

Flowering time: No flowers. Fertile fronds produce spores in late summer.

Foliage: Coiled copper shoots open as green fronds, turn gold in autumn.

Height: Up to 1.8m (6ft).

Spread: 1.2–1.8m (4–6ft).

Positioning: Full sun or moderate shade; in damp or wet, preferably acid, bog garden soil.

Care: Plant in spring, singly or 60–90cm (2–3ft) apart, in soil with added garden compost or leaf mould. Mulch after planting and repeat every autumn; feed with high-potash fertilizer in spring.

Propagation: Divide plants or remove outer portions with a spade in spring.

Recommended: Basic species; also crested 'Crispa' and 'Cristata', violet *purpurascens*.

Useful tip: Allow foliage to die down naturally, and clear in spring as new growth appears.

Related plants: *O. claytoniana*, young fronds pink; *O. cinnamomea*, brown woolly young growth.

OSMUNDA REGALIS

One of the largest and most decorative deciduous ferns, this is a native of river banks and other wet places, and provides an ideal edging for larger ponds. Although most ferns prefer cool shade, this species also enjoys sunny sites, where its seasonal colour changes are even more brilliant.

Peltandra undulata (Green) Arrow Arum

PELTANDRA UNDULATA

This robust arum reaches an impressive size, with individual leaves up to 90cm (3ft) long. A bold clump makes an excellent feature at the edge of a large still pond, especially when the 20cm (8in) high greenish-white flowers expand. They are followed by spikes of bright green berries. (syn. *P. virginica*.)

Flowering time: Early summer.

Foliage: Shiny, arrow-shaped and upright; deciduous in very cold gardens.

Height: 60cm (2ft).

Spread: 45cm (18in).

Positioning: Full sun or light shade; in wet soil in larger bog gardens or immersed to depth of 25cm (10in).

Care: Plant in spring, 30cm (12in) apart in natural groups, into the soil. Remove dead top growth in late autumn. In cold gardens cover plants grown on land with a deep layer of bracken or tree leaves.

Propagation: Divide creeping rhizomes in spring.

Recommended: Basic species only.

Useful tip: Plants are too large to grow in baskets, and prefer to spread freely in the bottom mud of larger ponds.

Related plants: *P. sagittifolia*, syn. *P. alba* (White Arrow Arum), less common species with pure white flowers and vivid red berries; very showy when grown with ferns and other contrasting foliage plants.

Pistia stratiotes Water Lettuce

Flowering time:	Summer (insignificant).
Foliage:	Thick, velvety and square-ended; in rosettes.
Height:	5–10cm (2–4in).
Spread:	30cm (12in) or more.
Positioning:	Full sun; at surface level in water 10–45cm (4–18in) deep.
Care:	Plant after the last spring frosts by floating rosettes in the water. Increase may be rapid in a warm season, but is easily controlled by removing young offsets from main plants. Transfer some young plants to trays of moist compost or tanks of water in early autumn, and overwinter indoors away from frost as insurance.
Propagation:	Cut off young plants from the ends of submerged side-shoots, and float in the pond immediately or keep indoors in an aquarium over winter.
Recommended:	Basic species only.
Useful tip:	Despite their common name, the plants are not edible.
Related plants:	None.

PISTIA STRATIOTES

A choice floating species, this is usually bought fresh each year to add an exotic element to ponds and also to provide a shelter for young water creatures. Found originally in the Nile river, it is a tropical plant and cannot survive frost, but with care it may be overwintered indoors.

Pontederia cordata Pickerel Weed

PONTEDERIA CORDATA

Blue flowers are desirable in any context, and this glorious water plant produces its welcome blue spikes late in the season, just when colour tends to dwindle in a pond. Plants may become invasive in shallow water and on land, so choose this species if you have a spacious pond.

Flowering time: Mid-summer to early autumn.

Foliage: Spear- or heart-shaped; upright in the water.

Height: 75–90cm (30–36in).

Spread: 45cm (18in).

Positioning: Full sun or very light shade; in very wet soil or immersed to depth of 10–38cm (4–15in).

Care: Plant in spring, singly in a wet bog garden or submerged in baskets, or 30cm (12in) apart in the soil at the bottom of larger ponds. Tidy dead foliage in autumn. Mulch crowns on land with tree leaves or bracken. Limit size where necessary by cutting back spreading roots in spring.

Propagation: Divide clumps in spring.

Recommended: Basic species and white form 'Alba'.

Useful tip: To help submerged plants survive the winter, make sure crowns are covered by at least 8–10cm (3–4in) of water.

Related plants: *P. c.* var. *lancifolia*, dark blue flowers; also *P. amphibia*, aquatic.

Flowering time: Spring, early summer.
Foliage: Soft, oval; in more or less evergreen rosettes.
Height: 30–90cm (12–36in).
Spread: 30–45cm (12–18in).
Positioning: Full sun or semi-shade; in rich moist, slightly acid, bog garden soil.
Care: Plant in autumn or spring, 15–23cm (6–9in) apart in natural groups, in soil with garden compost or leaf mould. Feed with general fertilizer in spring and mulch on drier sites. Divide every 4–5 years.
Propagation: Divide plants in autumn or spring or sow seeds in a cold frame in spring.
Recommended: P. Inshriach Hybrids (reddish-orange); P. japonica (pink); P. aurantiaca (bright orange); P. beesiana (rose-purple); P. pulverulenta (pink with dark eye).
Useful tip: Plants usually self-seed freely to produce mixed seedlings; deadhead after seeds disperse.
Related plants: Yellow P. florindae and P. sikkimensis, for wet soils.

PRIMULA FLORINDAE

A large group of mainly Asiatic primulas appreciate cool damp soils, and are therefore ideal candidates for a moist bog garden with leafy soil. There, the tall-stemmed flowers, many of them arranged in a series of whorls (Candelabra types), add their unique grace and beauty to the pond scene.

PULMONARIA SACCHARATA 'ARGENTEA'

These familiar cottage garden plants survive in dry soils but are happiest in moist shade, especially in more natural sites such as a wildlife bog gardens. More or less evergreen, their bold foliage is a good foil for the blue, red or white flowers and makes an efficient ground cover.

Flowering time:	Mid- to late spring.
Foliage:	Long and slender; often richly speckled.
Height:	30cm (12in).
Spread:	45cm (18in) or more.
Positioning:	Light or semi-shade; as edging and ground cover in moist but not waterlogged soil.
Care:	Plant in autumn or spring, 23–30cm (9–12in) apart in groups, in soil with plenty of garden compost or leaf mould. Mulch lightly in autumn and spring; feed in spring with general fertilizer. Remove dead leaves and trim creeping stems to size.
Propagation:	Divide plants in autumn or spring.
Recommended:	*P. saccharata* 'Mrs Moon'; *P. angustifolia*, especially 'Munstead Blue'; *P. longifolia* 'Bertram Anderson'; *P. officinalis* 'Sissinghurst White'; *P. rubra*.
Useful tip:	Combine with primulas, ferns and grasses.
Related plants:	*Mertensia* species are similar plants for moist shade.

Ranunculus acris Meadow Buttercup

Flowering time: Early summer to early autumn.

Foliage: Rounded, divided into several deep lobes; in a basal rosette.

Height: Up to 90cm (3ft).

Spread: 23–30cm (9–12in).

Positioning: Full sun or semi-shade; in a moist bog garden, especially beside wildlife ponds.

Care: Plant in autumn or spring, 23cm (9in) apart in natural drifts. Flower stems may need support with twiggy sticks. Cut down stems after flowering. Divide every 3–4 years.

Propagation: Divide clumps in autumn or spring.

Recommended: Double 'FLore Pleno', syn. 'Multiplex', and 'Stevenii'.

Useful tip: The long-stemmed flowers are excellent for indoor flower arrangements.

Related plants: R. aquatilis (Water Buttercup, Water Crowfoot), oxygenator for small ponds; R. fluitans for running water; R. lingua and smaller R. flammula are marginal plants for larger ponds.

RANUNCULUS ACRIS 'FLORE PLENO'

Although buttercups are usually regarded as weeds of moist meadows, and may not seem the ideal choice for a bog garden, this double form is an old cottage garden flower, much more restrained and perfect for naturalizing. Many other forms of Ranunculus deserve space, especially the very popular water buttercup.

Rheum palmatum Ornamental Rhubarb

RHEUM PALMATUM 'ATROSANGUINEUM'

A fast-growing species, ornamental rhubarb soon develops into a splendid mound of handsome foliage, especially in an open position away from competition. Beside still, reflective water the huge, richly coloured and finely incised leaves look stately; the 3m (10ft) plumes of red or purple flowers are even more imposing.

Flowering time:	Late spring and early summer.
Foliage:	Large, deeply cut; rich green or reddish-purple.
Height:	Up to 1.8m (6ft).
Spread:	1.5–1.8m (5–6ft) or more.
Positioning:	Full sun or semi-shade; in rich moist (not heavy) soil at the edge of larger ponds.
Care:	Plant in spring, in deeply dug soil with plenty of garden compost or well-rotted manure. Feed in spring with general fertilizer. Cut down top growth in autumn and mulch with garden compost, tree leaves or bracken; cover crowns thickly for winter protection.
Propagation:	Divide plants or cut off outer segments in spring.
Recommended:	Basic species and 'Atrosanguineum', 'Bowles' Crimson'.
Useful tip:	Divide clumps with a sharp spade or axe every 4–5 years where space is limited.
Related plants:	R. 'Ace of Hearts' is suitable for smaller ponds.

Rodgersia Rodgersia

Flowering time: Early and mid-summer.
Foliage: Large, lobed, crinkled; often red-tinted.
Height: 90cm–1.5m (3–5ft).
Spread: Up to 75cm (30in).
Positioning: Light or semi-shade; in rich moist soil beside larger ponds.
Care: Plant in autumn or spring, singly or 60cm (2ft) apart in groups of 3, in deeply dug soil with plenty of garden compost or leaf mould. Mulch in autumn; feed in spring with a high-potash fertilizer. Leave faded flowerheads over winter before cutting back.
Propagation: Divide plants in spring.
Recommended: R. podophylla 'Rotlaub' (purple leaves); R. aesculifolia (olive green palm-shaped leaves); R. pinnata 'Superba' (smaller; pink flowers).
Useful tip: Exposure to anything stronger than dappled sunlight scorches the leaves.
Related plants: R. tabularis, syn. Astilboides tabularis, huge leaves; a good hardy substitute for tender Gunnera.

RODGERSIA PINNATA 'SUPERBA'

These majestic foliage plants spread slowly and improve with age if left undisturbed. Their enormous leaves, up to 50–60cm (20–24in) wide, make efficient ground cover, even in moist woodland where plants are undeterred by tree roots. The elegant clusters of tiny flowers resemble those of astilbe, a close relative.

Sagittaria sagittifolia   Arrowhead

SAGITTARIA SAGITTIFOLIA

This handsome marginal plant for still shallow water is eye-catching with its gleaming arrow-head leaves. It is well-behaved if planted in large baskets but liable to be invasive elsewhere. In autumn the root tips develop starchy tubers, which are used for propagation and are also cultivated in Asia as a vegetable. (syn. *S. japonica*.)

Flowering time: Mid- and late summer.
Foliage: Bright green and arrow-shaped above water; long ribbons when submerged.
Height: 45-60cm (18-24in).
Spread: 30–45cm (12–18in).
Positioning: Full sun or light shade; in rich wet bog garden soil or immersed to depth of 30cm (12in).
Care: Plant in spring, singly or 23cm (9in) apart in groups, in baskets or into soil enriched with garden compost. Cut back dead growth in autumn. Divide every 2–3 years where growth is vigorous.
Propagation: Divide plants in spring or replant bulb-like tips of runners in autumn; sow seeds in trays of moist compost under glass in mid-spring.
Recommended: Basic species; also double-flowered 'Flore Pleno'.
Useful tip: Planting in deeper water reduces flowering.
Related plants: S. latifolia (Duck Potato), less hardy with large edible tubers; S. subulata, efficient oxygenating plant for deeper water.

Salix Willow

Flowering time: Spring (catkins).

Foliage: Long, slim; pale green or bluish, sometimes variegated.

Height: 90cm–3m (3–10ft).

Spread: 90cm–1.8m (3–6ft).

Positioning: Full sun or light shade; in damp or wet bog garden soil.

Care: Plant in autumn or winter, singly or 1.2m (4ft) apart in small groups, in soil enriched with garden compost or leaf mould. Stake taller willows until established. Mulch in autumn. In spring feed with general fertilizer and prune to shape.

Propagation: Grow 30cm (12in) cuttings in autumn or spring.

Recommended: S. alba sericea (silver); S. purpurea 'Gracilis' (dwarf Purple Willow); S. vitellina 'Britzensis', syn. 'Chermesina' (orange bark); S. integra 'Albo-marginata' (variegated), S. hookeriana.

Useful tip: Cut coloured-stemmed forms hard back in spring for new growth.

Related plants: Many other small Salix species.

SALIX HOOKERIANA

Willows are the most familiar waterside trees and shrubs, with a vast range of beautiful species that vary from tiny prostrate shrubs only 30cm (12in) high to majestic trees. For easy management in the average water garden, choose varieties that are less than about 3m (10ft) high and prune regularly.

Sasa veitchii   Kumazasa Bamboo

SASA VEITCHII

Bamboos are an essential ingredient of oriental water gardens, and exotic additions to any bog-plant scheme. They are graceful perennial grasses, mostly hardy and more or less evergreen. Many *Sasa* varieties have fascinating variations in stem and leaf colour. Choose bamboos carefully, though, as some of them can be very invasive.

Flowering time: Summer (rare).
Foliage: Long, slim, pointed; often variegated.
Height: Up to 2.4m (8ft).
Spread: 60–90cm (2–3ft) or more.
Positioning: Full sun or semi-shade; in moist but not waterlogged bog garden soil where spreading roots can be controlled.
Care: Plant in early spring or early autumn, in deeply dug soil enriched with garden compost or well-rotted manure, and protect with a 10cm (4in) mulch. Feed in spring with general fertilizer. Remove damaged or dead stems in autumn. Cut back spreading varieties with a spade in summer.
Propagation: Divide clumps in early or mid-summer.
Recommended: Basic species and shorter *minor*.
Useful tip: Water often if the first year of growth is dry.
Related plants: *Pleioblastus auricomus*, yellow-striped leaves, 1.2m (4ft); *Indocalamus tessellatus*, syn. *Sasa tessellata*, 2.4m (8ft).

Saururus cernuus   Lizard's Tail, American Swamp Lily

Flowering time: Early to late summer.
Foliage: Large and heart-shaped, olive green; turns crimson in autumn.
Height: 1.2m (4ft).
Spread: 60cm–1.2m (2–4ft).
Positioning: Full sun or semi-shade; in wet bog garden soil or immersed to depth of 10cm (4in).
Care: Plant in spring, singly or 45cm (18in) apart in small groups, into the soil or in baskets. Mulch plants grown on land with garden compost in autumn; feed in spring with general fertilizer. Cut down all growth in autumn. Divide every 4–5 years.
Propagation: Divide clumps in spring.
Recommended: Basic species only.
Useful tip: Plants remain small when immersed in baskets, but may exceed 1.2m (4ft) high when allowed free run in a bog garden.
Related plants: S. chinensis, similar species with ivory flowers. Also Houttuynia cordata, a close relative.

SAURURUS CERNUUS

Wet bog gardens and still shallow water both suit this North American perennial, which is well-behaved when grown in a planting basket but often invasive if left to grow unchecked. The prolific foliage assumes brilliant tints in autumn, and the gracefully arching heads of fluffy white flowers have a unique appeal.

Schizostylis coccinea · River Lily, Kaffir Lily

SCHIZOSTYLIS COCCINEA 'MAJOR'

These gorgeous late-flowering perennials come from South Africa, where they are always called river lilies – appropriately, because they normally grow beside streams and in shallow moving water. The simple species is very vigorous and only suitable for larger ponds and bog gardens, whereas hybrids are more restrained.

Flowering time: Early autumn to early winter.

Foliage: Long, narrow, grassy; in vigorous clumps.

Height: 60cm (24in).

Spread: 25–30cm (10–12in).

Positioning: Full sun, sheltered from strong winds and hard frost; in moist or wet bog garden soil or immersed to depth of 10cm (4in).

Care: Plant rhizomes in spring, 25cm (10in) apart in natural groups, at the edge of medium-size or large ponds. Mulch plants grown on land in autumn; feed in spring with general fertilizer.

Propagation: Separate young offshoots from main plants in spring.

Recommended: Basic species; also hybrids such as *alba*, 'Major' (bright rose pink), 'Professor Barnard' (dark red), 'Sunrise' (salmon pink), 'November Cheer' (light pink).

Useful tip: In cold gardens, protect crowns from winter frosts with a layer of straw or tree leaves.

Related plants: None.

Schoenoplectus lacustris Club Rush

Flowering time: Early summer to early autumn.

Foliage: Long and rounded; in robust clumps.

Height: 90cm–3m (3–10ft).

Spread: 60–90cm (2–3ft).

Positioning: Full sun or light shade; in wet soil or immersed to depth of 30cm (12in).

Care: Plant in spring, singly or 30cm (12in) apart in groups, into soil or in baskets. Mulch plants grown on land in autumn; feed all plants in spring with a general fertilizer.

Propagation: Divide clumps in spring.

Recommended: Basic species; also S. l. tabernaemontii and variegated 'Albescens' and 'Zebrinus'; dwarf Scirpus mucronatus, with horizontal flowers, and S. 'Golden Flower'.

Useful tip: Grow in containers in formal gardens for ease of maintenance.

Related plants: Eleocharis dulcis (Chinese Water Chestnut), slightly tender; Scirpoides holoschoenus (Round-headed Club Rush), for small ponds.

SCHOENOPLECTUS LACUSTRIS 'ZEBRINUS'

This is the bulrush of streams and river shallows, a tall and vigorous plant suitable for the largest wildlife ponds and bog gardens. Where space is more limited, grow S. l. tabernaemontii or one of the popular striped varieties, which make excellent specimen plants for small ponds. (syn. Scirpus lacustris.)

Stratiotes aloides Water Soldier

STRATIOTES ALOIDES

This intriguing plant resembles a floating pineapple-top with stiff toothed leaves arranged in a rosettes. It roots out of sight in shallow water, especially in winter when plants remain at the bottom as a valuable carpet of oxygenating foliage.

Flowering time: Early to mid-summer.

Foliage: Sharply pointed, dark olive green; in a floating rosette. More or less evergreen.

Height: 30–38cm (12–15in).

Spread: 60cm (24in).

Positioning: Full sun or very light shade; in still water 30–90cm (1–3ft) deep.

Care: Plant in spring: allow young rosettes to float freely in shallow water. Plants sink and multiply when they have flowered and surface again in late summer, when surplus offsets can be thinned with a net.

Propagation: Separate young plants in spring and summer.

Recommended: Basic species only.

Useful tip: As an insurance against losses in cold weather, keep a few young plants in jars of soil and water indoors over winter.

Related plants: *Hydrocleys nymphoides*, syn. *Stratiotes nymphoides*, yellow flowers; for indoor pools or warm outdoor ponds in summer only.

Flowering time: Mid- to late summer.

Foliage: Lozenge-shaped; bright green turning orange-red in autumn; on inflated stems in a floating rosette.

Height: 5cm (2in).

Spread: Up to 45cm (18in); submerged shoots up to 4m (13ft) in frost-free ponds.

Positioning: Full sun; in still water 30–75cm (12–30in) deep, ideally above a muddy bottom.

Care: Plant in late spring after the last serious frosts: disperse young rosettes on the surface. In warmer districts, it may be necessary to thin plants by removing runners and their young offsets.

Propagation: Separate young rosettes (offsets) in summer.

Recommended: Basic species only.

Useful tip: Plants need supplementary light and heat to survive winter indoors, but ripe fruits can be kept in cold water in frost-free conditions for planting in spring after the last frosts.

Related plants: None.

TRAPA NATANS

Although strictly perennial, these plants are normally grown as annuals as they cannot withstand frost. However, the spiny fruits survive on the muddy bottom of ponds or can be collected and kept indoors. These edible fruits are part of Indian cuisine (the familiar Chinese water chestnut is a different species, *Eleocharis dulcis*).

Trollius europaeus Globe Flower

TROLLIUS 'SUPERBUS'

Daintier than the large-flowered cultivated forms, this is the wild globe flower and adds a special grace and charm to wildflower bog gardens. It is not invasive and looks most effective when planted in natural drifts among astilbes and ferns, or on its own in a rock garden.

Flowering time: Late spring and early summer.

Foliage: Rich green; divided like a buttercup.

Height: 45–75cm (18–30in).

Spread: 30–45cm (12–18in).

Positioning: Full sun or light shade; in moist or wet bog garden soil and waterside rockeries.

Care: Plant in autumn or spring, 23cm (9in) apart in small groups. Feed in spring with general fertilizer and mulch with garden compost or leaf mould. Divide every 3–4 years.

Propagation: Divide clumps in autumn or spring.

Recommended: Basic species and hybrids such as 'Superbus'.

Useful tip: Deadheading as soon as blooms fade sometimes encourages a late second flowering.

Related plants: Cultivated forms suitable for bog gardens include *T.* × *cultorum* 'Canary Bird', 'Fire Globe', 'Golden Cup' and 'Orange Princess'; *T. pumilus* is a dwarf species for small ponds.

Flowering time: Early to late summer.

Foliage: Long and ribbon-like; semi-evergreen in a cold winter.

Height: 45cm–3m (18in–10ft).

Spread: 90cm (3ft).

Positioning: Full sun or very light shade; in moist or wet bog garden soil or immersed to depth of 30cm (12in).

Care: Plant in spring, 60cm (2ft) apart in groups in the soil or singly in baskets. Deadhead if seeding is unwelcome. Remove dead foliage at the end of winter. Divide every 3–4 years.

Propagation: Divide clumps in spring.

Recommended: *T. angustifolia* (Lesser Bulrush) and *T. laxmannii*, medium height; *T. latifolia* (Common Cattail), especially 'Variegata' (yellow stripes); *T. minima*, a miniature species for small ponds.

Useful tip: In garden ponds all species are best confined to baskets to restrict their creeping rhizomes.

Related plants: None.

TYPHA LAXMANNII

These familiar pond and streamside plants, often mistakenly called bulrushes, are distinctive with their cigar-shaped female flower spikes (the male blooms form a tuft above the 'bulrush'). Their creeping rhizomes can be invasive and most species are best suited to larger wildlife ponds.

Utricularia vulgaris Greater Bladderwort

UTRICULARIA VULGARIS

This intriguing oxygenator floats as a tangled mass, mostly just below the surface of the water. In summer, the attractive yellow or golden-orange flowers emerge from the water, looking like small speckled antirrhinums. The plants have no roots and subsist by catching tiny aquatic organisms in the minute insectivorous bladders that stud the stems.

Flowering time: Mid- and late summer.

Foliage: Dark green and thread-like; in tangled submerged masses.

Height: Flowers up to 23cm (9in).

Spread: Up to 60cm (2ft).

Positioning: Full sun or semi-shade; in still water of any depth, preferably lime-free.

Care: Plant in spring: float young plants on the pond surface once the water has begun to warm up. After 1–2 seasons, clumps may need thinning in summer. Plants disappear in winter and survive as dormant buds and stem fragments on the pond bottom.

Propagation: Divide the mass of stems in spring or summer.

Recommended: Basic species only.

Useful tip: Choose related species with care as most are terrestrial, or tropical and unlikely to survive in a pond.

Related plants: *U. minor* (Lesser Bladderwort), smaller with dainty yellow blooms; *U. purpurea*, rose pink flowers.

Flowering time: Late spring to early autumn.

Foliage: Oval and glossy, on sprawling stems; normally deciduous but evergreen below water.

Height: 15cm (6in).

Spread: 45–60cm (18–24in).

Positioning: Full sun or semi-shade; in wet soil in bog gardens, on pond banks or immersed to depth of 20cm (8in).

Care: Plant in spring, 30cm (12in) apart in small groups, into the soil or in baskets if immersed. Trim back prostrate rooting stems in autumn or whenever the plants become invasive.

Propagation: Divide plants in spring, or detach rooted stems in spring and summer.

Recommended: Basic species only.

Useful tip: The young shoots of the plant are edible.

Related plants: V. anagallis-aquatica (Water Pimpernel); V. scutellata (Marsh Speedwell), white or pink; V. virginica, syn. Veronicastrum virginicum (Culver's Root).

VERONICA BECCABUNGA

This cheerful species for wildflower bog gardens and natural ponds would be much taller if its stems would only stand upright. Their normal habit is to sprawl lazily, often rooting wherever they touch the ground, and then turn upwards at the tips. The blue flowers appear along the full length of the stems over a long season.

Zantedeschia aethiopica Arum Lily, Calla Lily

Flowering time: Spring, early summer.

Foliage: Large and glossy, on long stalks; sometimes variegated.

Height: 45–60cm (18–24in).

Spread: 30–38cm (12–15in).

Positioning: Full sun or semi-shade; in wet bog garden soil or immersed to depth of 30cm (12in).

Care: Plant in spring, singly or 25cm (10in) apart in small groups, into soil or in baskets. Dig up plants in autumn and keep indoors in pots. In mild areas cover plants grown on land with a thick mulch of straw or tree leaves; immersed ones will be safe under 23–25cm (9–10in) of water.

Propagation: Divide plants in spring.

Recommended: Basic species, slightly hardier form 'Crowborough' and tender 'Green Goddess' (variegated).

Useful tip: Plants may be grown in large pots, buried outdoors in spring and brought inside in autumn.

Related plants: Most other forms and hybrids are too tender for outdoor ponds.

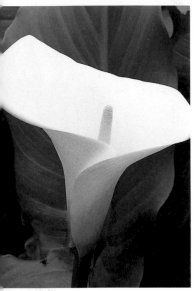

ZANTEDESCHIA AETHIOPICA

Perhaps more familiar as house plants, arum or calla lilies are natural candidates for bog gardens and the margins of larger ponds, provided they are protected against severe frost, preferably under water, or brought indoors for the winter. They are most effective in bold clumps that are kept separate as highlights.